Bilingual Edition

READING POWER

Edición Bilingüe

Extreme Machines

Low Riders

Autos low rider

Scott P. Werther

The Rosen Publishing Group's

PowerKids Press™ & **Buenas Letras**™

New York

1

Published in 2003 by The Rosen Publishing Group, Inc.
29 East 21st Street, New York, NY 10010
Copyright © 2003 by The Rosen Publishing Group, Inc.

First Bilingual Edition 2003
First Edition in English 2002

Book Design: Michelle Innes
Photo Credits: © Jack Parsons

Werther , Scott P
Low Riders/Autos "lowrider"/Scott P. Werther ; traducción al español:
Spanish Educational Publishing
p. cm. — (Extreme Machines)
Includes bibliographical references and index.
ISBN 0-8239-6888-X (lib. bdg.)
1. Low riders—Juvenile literature. [1. Low riders 2. Automoviles-Customizing.
3. Spanish Language Materials—Bilingual.] I. Title.
TG106.K63 T48 2001
624'.5—dc21

                                                2001000599

Manufactured in the United States of America

Contents _____

_____ Contenido

This is a low rider. It is an old car that has been made low to the ground.

Éste es un auto low rider.
Es un auto antiguo
al que se baja la carrocería
para acercarlo al suelo.

This low rider is a car
from 1963.

Este low rider es un auto de 1963.

This low rider is very long.

Este auto es muy largo.

This low rider is very old.

Este auto es muy antiguo.

This is the inside of a low rider.

_____

Así es este low rider por dentro.

Some low riders have fancy paint jobs like this one.

Algunos de estos autos están decorados con diseños muy bonitos.

This low rider has lifts at the wheels that make the front and the back of the car go up and down. The back of this low rider is down.

Este auto tiene piezas especiales
en las ruedas.
Suben y bajan la parte de
adelante y de atrás. La parte de
atrás de este auto está bajada.

The back of this low
rider is up.

La parte de atrás de este auto
está subida.

Low riders can also be trucks. This low rider truck has gold flames on the side.

También hay camionetas
low rider. Esta camioneta está
decorada con llamas.

Glossary

fancy (**fan**-see) something that is made to look nice

flame (**flaym**) the part of a fire that you can see shoot up into the air

lift (**lihft**) something that makes things go up and down

low rider (**loh ry**-duhr) a car that is made to be close to the ground

Glosario

carrocería (**la**) cuerpo de un auto o camioneta

llama (**la**) parte del fuego que sube en el aire

low rider (**el**) auto antiguo al que se baja la carrocería para que esté más cerca del suelo

pieza (**la**) parte de un auto o camioneta

Resources / Recursos

Here are more books to read about low riders:
Otros libros que puedes leer sobre autos lowrider:

Eyewitness: Car
by Richard Sutton, Dave King, Mike Dunning
Dorling Kindersley Publishing (2000)

Classic American Cars
by Quentin Willson, Matthew Ward
Dorling Kindersley Publishing (1997)

Word count in English: 110
Número de palabras en español: 102

Index

Índice